Spiritu[al]
Warfare for
Kingdom Kids

Sherry Grandfield

Spiritual Warfare for Kingdom Kids

Trilogy Christian Publishers A Wholly Owned Subsidary of Trinity Broadcasting Network

2442 Michelle Drive Tustin, CA 92780

Rights Department, 2442 Michelle Drive, Tustin, CA 92780.

Trilogy Christian Publishing/TBN and colophon are trademarks of Trinity Broadcasting Network.

For information about special discounts for bulk purchases, please contact Trilogy Christian Publishing.

Trilogy Disclaimer: The views and content expressed in this book are those of the author and may not necessarily reflect the views and doctrine of Trilogy Christian Publishing or the Trinity Broadcasting Network.

Manufactured in the United States of America

10 9 8 7 6 5 4 3 2 1

Library of Congress Cataloging-in-Publication Data is available.

ISBN: 978-1-64773-284-4

E-ISBN: 978-1-64773-285-1

Table of Contents

Introduction

When you go out to battle against your enemies and see horses and chariots and people more numerous than you, do not be afraid of them; for the Lord, your God, who brought you up from the land of Egypt is with you. When you approach the battle, the priest shall come forward and speak to the people and shall say to them, "Hear, O Israel: you are advancing today to battle against your enemies. Do not lack courage. Do not be afraid, or panic, or tremble [in terror] before them, for the LORD your God is He who goes with you, to fight for you against your enemies, to save you" (Deuteronomy 20:1-4, AMP).

So, we are in the middle of Star Wars, yet most people don't know it. You won't see it unless you are actually paying attention. You will notice the set-ups if you are truly paying attention to your everyday occurrences. The coincidences that happen are often not "good" coincidences, especially within our public schools.

This book is to teach you how to fight the system of darkness, created from the kingdom of darkness, overseen by the prince of the power of the air. I promise to make everything clear, simple, concise and to the point. I am not going to dilly-dally around with theory or anecdotes. I taught in public schools for 15 years and was a reading teacher/reading coach for most of that time. So, I know how to make things easy so everyone can understand and succeed.

My goal is to give you the best instruction and the best resources that I know of, so you can surpass my achievement level and go on to teach others how to fight the system of darkness and win. There is only one way. I'm not here to argue that point. If you follow the instructions you are given in this book, then you will win.

Before you read Assessment

I always like to figure out what I know about something new before I read about it. After I read about what used to be new, I then like to see what I learned. This is called an ABC list and it's an easy way to see your growth at the end of the reading. List all the letters of the alphabet down the side of a paper or in two columns. Think about the title of this book: Spiritual Warfare for Kingdom Kids. Write one word that starts with each letter of the alphabet that you think relates to the title. If you can't think of one, leave it blank. This should only take about 15 minutes or less.

A _Angles_

B _Betrayed_

C _Conflict_

D _Dark/decision_

E mortal

F ight

G bod

H Holy Holy Holy

I nter in "I will"

J Jesus

K indom

L ove

M ind

N asty

O pen your heart

P erswation

Q uit

R un

S ee

T _Trinity_

U _under_

V _eracity_

W _arfare_

X _____

Y _es_

Z _____

Now you should have a good idea about what you know about this topic. Another thing I like to do is compare it with a reading buddy or a group of three to four, if a few of your friends are reading the same book. How you use this tool is up to you. Be Blessed.

Sherry Grandfield

Step One: Get Saved

"For we walk by faith, not by sight [living our lives in a manner consistent with our confident belief in God's promises] we are [as I was saying] of good courage and confident hope, and I prefer rather to be absent from the body and to be at home with the Lord" (2 Corinthians 5:7-8, AMP).

Get saved. What's that you ask? What does that mean?

Basically, it is this:

Accept Jesus Christ as your Lord and Savior.

Why is that necessary? I know my thoughts concerning this, at the age of 10 were:

1. Doesn't God love everyone?

2. If so, then why do we need to do anything?

I was approached one day by my younger brother's friend to take Jesus into my heart. She lived down the street and was five or six years old at the time. She was Baptist. I didn't get saved that day because what she asked me to do didn't make sense to me. I asked her those very questions and she had no answer for me. I have the answers now; although I didn't get the answers until many years had passed. Thank God for his mercy.

The answers are quite simple. Jesus is the only one who can give us eternal life. He is the only one who can truly protect us from the kingdom of darkness. I know you might be thinking, "Well, aren't there other ways to be protected? What about the angels? What about wizards? What about Santeros? White witches? Crystals? Protective jewelry" The lists of worldly protections are endless.

The only angels that can assist you are the ones from the Kingdom of God under the authority of Jesus Christ. As far as the other beings or objects they cannot protect you. They are the works and representations of the kingdom of darkness. Remember, I am not here to debate or argue. I am just here to speak the truth and tell you the right and basic steps to be successful in spiritual warfare. "In the beginning (before all time) was The Word (Christ), and The Word was with God, and The Word was God Himself"

(John 1:1, AMP).

> He was [continually existing] in the beginning [co-eternally] with God. All things were made *and* came into existence through Him, and without Him, not even one thing was made that has come into being. In Him was life [and the power to bestow life], and the life was the Light of men. The Light shines on in the darkness, and the darkness did not understand it or overpower it or absorb it [and is unreceptive to it].

> John 1:2-6 (AMP)

The word is Jesus, and Christ is the Greek word for "the Anointed One." He is the only one who came to the earth and died on the cross as a perfect sacrifice and was raised in three days from the dead. He fulfilled the scriptures in the Old Testament in the book of Isaiah. He is Isaiah 61:1-2 in the flesh. He went to hell and made a mockery of the kingdom of darkness and then ascended to Heaven to sit at the right hand of God: The Father.

> The Spirit of the Sovereign Lord is upon me, for the Lord has anointed me to bring good news to the poor. He has sent me to comfort the brokenhearted and to proclaim that captives will be released and prisoners will be freed. He has sent me to tell those who mourn that the time of the Lord's favor has come, and with it, the day of God's anger against their enemies.
>
> Isaiah 61:1-2 (AMP)

Jesus preached the words of Isaiah 61:1-2 everywhere he went. Through Jesus, we can have the same spirit in us and upon us.

"And if the Spirit of Him who raised Jesus from the dead lives in you, He who raised Christ Jesus from the dead will also give life to your mortal bodies through His Spirit, who lives in you" (Romans 8:11, AMP).

The first step to get that same spirit is to get saved! Ok, so how do I get saved? I am so glad you asked. I'm going to give you the best salvation prayer I've found.

"Salvation Prayer"

"Heavenly Father, I believe that Jesus died on the cross for me and was raised in three days from the dead. I now ask Jesus to come into my heart to be my Lord, master and savior. Satan, I renounce you and no longer serve you. Jesus is my Master. Thank you, Jesus, for saving me, in Jesus' name I pray. Amen."

For more clarity about why Jesus is the only way: it's because of the cross. He is the only one to die on the cross and be the perfect sacrifice to ensure all of our sins are covered. There are people who practice Voodoo, witchcraft, do blood sacrifices to demi-gods, saints, and whatever else they call them. Jesus sacrificed himself to the one and only father of Abraham, Isaac and Jacob, that is why his name is above *every* name.

Important ideas, Notes, and Words to clarify:

_____

_____

_____

Step Two: Get Baptized

"He who has believed [in Me] and has been baptized will be saved [from the penalty of God's wrath and judgment]; but he who has not believed will be condemned" (Mark 16:16, AMP).

Baptism is important. I believe you need to be baptized in water (full immersion) and by fire (with the Holy Spirit). Baptism in water can be done in any body of water. Baptism in water can take place in a bathtub, a pool, a lake, the sea, the ocean, in a river; the type of water doesn't matter. It is an outward expression of giving up the old ways, the stuff of the world. You go down and under one way and come up a new creature in Christ (The Anointed One).

> As for me, I baptize you with water because of [your] repentance [that is, because you are willing to change your inner self—your old way of thinking, regret your sin, and live a changed life], but He (the Messiah) who is coming after me is mightier than I, whose sandals I am not worthy to remove [even as His

slave]; He will baptize you [who truly repent] with the Holy Spirit and [you who remain unrepentant] with fire (judgment). His winnowing fork is in His hand, and He will thoroughly clear out His threshing floor, and He will gather His wheat (believers) into His barn (kingdom), but He will burn up the chaff (the unrepentant) with unquenchable fire.

Matthew 3: 11-12 (AMP)

Where can I get baptized you ask? Who can baptize me? I am so glad you asked!!

Many people get baptized at a church or with a church at a location with a body of water; however, you can be baptized by any believer or disciple of Christ. God is your witness and he knows your heart. The point is you are outwardly surrendering your complete self to God and becoming a new creature in Christ (The Anointed One).

Therefore, if anyone is in Christ [that is, grafted in, joined to Him by faith in Him as Savior], *he is* a new creature [reborn and renewed by the Holy Spirit]; the old things [the previous moral and spiritual condition] have passed away. Behold, new things have come [because spiritual awakening brings a new life].

2 Corinthians 5:7 (AMP)

"Depart, depart, go out from there (the lands of exile), Touch no unclean thing; go out of the midst of her (Babylon), purify yourselves, you who carry the articles of the LORD [on your journey from there]" (Isaiah 52:11, AMP).

In the Appendix at the back of this book, there will be a list of resources. If you currently do not belong to a church, then pray for God to lead you to the right one *for you*. God will honor your prayers. God is omniscient (all-knowing) and he has a perfect plan for your life so you can fulfill your perfect purpose and destiny. He will provide for you in every area as you surrender to him.

Your last question may be, "What if someone is not baptized?" For example, someone is in the hospital or an ambulance, accepts Jesus, and then immediately expires. God will honor them and accept them into The Kingdom. Our God is a God of mercy. However, since he so purely loves us as his children, we should do all we can to honor him in our lives in every way possible. Water baptism is a very important way to honor our God.

Important ideas, Notes, and Words to clarify:

_____

_____

_____

_____

_____

_____

_____

_____

_____

_____

_____

_____

_____

_____

_____

_____

_____

_____

_____

_____

_____

_____

_____

_____

Step Three: Baptism by Fire

After or before water baptism, it is extremely important to get baptized by the Holy Spirit, also known as "baptism by fire." This is where God gives you the power and authority over demons, the demonic realm, and the kingdom of darkness. Why is it referred to as "baptism by fire"? Please read the scripture below which is the first reference in the Bible to people receiving the Holy Spirit.

> When the day of Pentecost had come, they were all together in one place, and suddenly a sound came from Heaven like a rushing violent wind, and it filled the whole house where they were sitting. There appeared to them tongues resembling fire, which were being distributed [among them], and they rested on each one of them [as each person received the Holy Spirit]. And they were all filled [that is, diffused throughout their being] with the Holy Spirit and began to speak in other tongues (different languages), as the Spirit was giving them the ability to speak out [clearly and appropriately].
>
> Acts 2:1-4 (AMP)

Your next question may be "How do I get baptized in the Holy Spirit?" and I am happy to answer this question. The more people that receive this gift, the better everything will be for everyone. A person can receive the Holy Spirit by simply asking God for it. I have also seen people receive the Holy Spirit being prayed for by others who have the Holy Spirit.

This is how it happened for me:

I was at a service with a special speaker. There was an altar call and I always went up. I knew I needed help, and I was grateful for whatever help God wanted to give me. On this day, the pastor who was speaking looked into my eyes and instructed me to say, "I submit to the Holy Spirit." I did as requested. I will tell you, the very instant I said those words, the entire atmosphere around me shifted. Everything changed in my life that day. I have never felt the same.

I did not receive my heavenly prayer language that day, but I believe it set me on the course to have it. I personally received my gift of speaking in tongues while watching a service on Trinity Broadcasting Network. The preacher said the baptism of the Holy Spirit (speaking in tongues) gives you power over demons. I said to myself, "Well I need that." Then he said, "If you would like the baptism, just put your hands out towards the TV," and he began

to pray for us to receive the baptism. I reached out towards the

screen, I felt electricity flow towards me, and I fell back onto my

bed. Then, three days later, I woke up speaking in tongues. Below

you will see a prayer to receive the best gift one could ever have.

"Heavenly Father, in the name of Jesus, The Anointed One, I

humbly ask to be baptized in the Holy Spirit of the Living God.

I thank you, Father, for the gift of the baptism of the Holy Spirit

with evidence of speaking with new tongues, in Jesus' name.

Amen."

> These signs will accompany those who have believed:
> in My name, they will cast out demons, they will
> speak in new tongues; they will pick up serpents, and
> if they drink anything deadly, it will not hurt them;
> they will lay hands on the sick, and they will get well.

> Mark 16:17-19 (AMP)

You will know you have received the baptism because you

will speak in another language. This language is also referred to as

the "language of angels." It will be unknown to you, but it is your

spirit communicating with the Holy Spirit. It is the perfect prayer

language as it is direct communication with God. This too will be

explained more in-depth through the suggested resources. For right

now, it is best just to ask the Lord to baptize you in the Holy Spirit or ask for the baptism of fire. God knows what you are asking for and he will answer you.

Important ideas, Notes, and Words to clarify:

_____

_____

_____

_____

_____

_____

_____

_____

_____

_____

_____

_____

_____

_____

_____

_____

Step Four: Command Your Morning

Witches and warlocks are up praying after midnight and many more praying heavily between the hours of 3:00 and 6:00 in the wee hours of the morning; therefore, it is a good habit to pray at those times as well. I know you may be sleeping but, if you do wake up during that time frame, even for a few minutes, then take a moment or more to pray before going back to sleep. Commanding your morning praise will dislodge those going out from the kingdom of darkness. I know to some of you, this may sound far out, but the forces of evil do exist in this realm.

There are many prayers to pray to command your morning. As time goes on, you will develop your own, personal prayers. The resources section will include books and websites where prayers may be found. However, I believe the best prayer to start your day and the best prayer to say at any time is straight from Jesus, The

Anointed One, Himself:

> Pray then, in this way:
> "Our Father, who is in Heaven,
> Hallowed be your name.
> Your Kingdom come
> Your Will be done
> On earth
> As it is in Heaven.
> Give us this day our daily
> bread.
> And forgive us our debts, as
> we forgive our debtors
> [letting go of both the wrong and
> the resentment].
> And do not lead us into
> temptation, but deliver us from
> evil. [For Yours is the kingdom
> and the power and the glory
> forever. Amen.]"
>
> Matthew 6:9-13 (AMP)

Another wonderful scripture to pray when starting your day is Ephesians 1:2-3. I also suggest you personalize the scripture to yourself or someone you are praying for privately. Grace...and peace [inner calm and spiritual well-being] from God our Father and the Lord Jesus Christ *be mine*. Blessed *and* worthy of praise be the God and Father of our Lord Jesus Christ, who has blessed *me (your name)* with every spiritual blessing in the heavenly realms in Christ (Ephesians 1:2-3, AMP, author's paraphrase).

Here I would like to point out that Messiah also means "The Anointed One" just as Christ is Greek for "The Anointed One." So, if every time you remember to read it as "The Anointed One" when you see either the Messiah or Christ, the Bible will have more revelatory meaning to you.

Important ideas, Notes, and Words to clarify:

_____

_____

_____

_____

_____

_____

_____

_____

_____

_____

_____

_____

_____

_____

_____

Sherry Grandfield

_____

_____

_____

_____

_____

_____

_____

_____

_____

_____

_____

_____

_____

_____

_____

_____

_____

_____

_____

_____

_____

_____

_____

Step Five: Put on the Whole Armor of God

Putting on the whole armor of God is referred to often in the church. This phrase or instruction is practiced or believed to mean so many things in the body of Christ. I don't agree with all of them. I will tell you what I know to be true. If someone is sending witchcraft to you and you feel it overtaking you, (sudden dizziness, nausea, or a sudden sharp unexplainable pain), then you can have instant protection with this armor. All you have to do is say a simple prayer. This prayer made a world of difference in my everyday life:

Thank you, Father, for putting the complete armor of God on me, right now in Jesus' name. Amen.

I learned this in a book entitled *Prepare for War* by Rebecca Brown, MD, Dr. Brown had come out of witchcraft and began serving God and still does today. Unfortunately, I had been involved in many occult practices before finding God. Maybe you also have done so unknowingly by reading and believing horoscopes, playing with a Ouija board, playing with Tarot Cards, seeing a fortune teller or psychic, reading fiction books about witchcraft, vampires, etc.

The armor of God is also described in the Bible with full spiritual meaning, and Apostle Paul instructs us to put it on daily. I've heard other Christians say once you put it on you can leave it on. If that were the case, I believe Apostle Paul would have said so. I have had to use it against witchcraft by praying the prayer mentioned above. My recommendation is that we all say that little prayer every day before stepping outside of our home.

> In conclusion, be strong in the Lord [draw your strength from Him and be empowered through your union with Him] and in the power of His [boundless] might. Put on the full armor of God [for His precepts are like the splendid armor of a heavily armed soldier], so that you may be able to [successfully] stand up against all the schemes *and* the strategies *and* the deceits of the devil. For our struggle is not against flesh and blood [contending only with physical opponents], but against the rulers, against the powers, against the world forces of this [present] darkness, against the spiritual forces of wickedness in the heavenly (supernatural places. Therefore, put on the complete armor of God, so that you will be able to [successfully] resist *and* stand your ground in

the evil day [of danger], and having done everything [that the crisis demands], to stand firm [in your place, fully prepared, immovable, victorious].

Ephesians 6:10-13 (AMP)

When you are in a war, you need armor. Roman soldiers had armor of metal from head to toe. Soldiers today wear body armor which covers the upper body, torso and pelvic area. The armor of God covers us from head to toe—with no breaks in between. We may not see it, but our enemies cannot penetrate it. Hallelujah Jesus! Hallelujah! Hallelujah! Hallelujah!

Important ideas, Notes, and Words to clarify:

_____

_____

_____

_____

_____

_____

_____

_____

_____

_____

Step Six: Memorize your Sword

You will hear people say, "Where is your sword?" referring to your Bible. The word of God is a mighty weapon when applied to any situation. I will give you the three parts of the Bible that I memorized first. They are used for protection which is very necessary for spiritual warfare. Memorizing Psalm 91, Isaiah 54:17, and Psalm 23 is a great place to begin.

> He who dwells in the shelter of the Most High
> Will remain secure *and* rest in the shadow of the
> Almighty [whose power no enemy can withstand].
> I will say of the LORD, "He is my refuge and my
> fortress,
> My God, in whom I trust [with great confidence,
> and on whom I rely]!"
> For He will save you from the trap of the fowler,
> And from the deadly pestilence.
> He will cover you *and* completely protect you with
> His pinions,
> And under His wings you will find refuge;

His faithfulness is a shield and a wall.
You will not be afraid of the terror of night,
Nor of the arrow that flies by day,
Nor of the pestilence that stalks in darkness,
Nor of the destruction (sudden death) that lays
waste at noon.
A thousand may fall at your side
And ten thousand at your right hand,
But danger will not come near you.
You will only [be a spectator as you] look on with
your eyes
And witness the [divine] repayment of the wicked
[as you watch safely from the shelter of the Most
High].
Because you have made the LORD, [who is] my
refuge,
Even the Most High, your dwelling place,
No evil will befall you,
Nor will any plague come near your tent.
For He will command His angels in regard to you,
To protect *and* defend *and* guard you in all your
ways [of obedience and service].
They will lift you up in their hands,
So that you do not [even] strike your foot against a
stone.
You will tread upon the lion and cobra;
The young lion and the serpent you will trample
underfoot.
"Because he set his love on Me, therefore I will
save him;
I will set him [securely] on high, because he knows
My name [he confidently trusts and relies on Me,
knowing I will never abandon him, no, never].
"He will call upon Me, and I will answer him;
I will be with him in trouble;
I will rescue him and honor him.
"With a long life I will satisfy him

And I will let him see My salvation."

Psalm 91 (AMP)

"No weapon that is formed against you will
succeed; And every tongue that rises against
you in judgment you will condemn. This [peace,
righteousness, security, and triumph over
opposition] is the heritage of the servants of
the LORD, And *this is* their vindication from Me,"
says the LORD.

Isaiah 54:17 (AMP)

The LORD is my Shepherd [to feed, to guide, and
to shield me], I shall not want. He lets me lie
down in green pastures; He leads me beside the
still *and* quiet waters. He refreshes *and* restores my
soul (life); He leads me in the paths of righteousness
for His name's sake. Even though I walk through
the [sunless] valley of the shadow of death, I fear no
evil, for You are with me;
Your rod [to protect] and Your staff [to guide], they
comfort *and* console me.
You prepare a table before me in the presence of
my enemies. You have anointed *and* refreshed my
head with oil; My cup overflows. Surely goodness
and mercy *and* unfailing love shall follow me
all the days of my life, And I shall dwell forever
[throughout all my days] in the house *and* in the
presence of the LORD.

Psalm 23 (AMP)

I am led at this time by the Holy Spirit to now include The

King James Version of the same Psalm 91 and Psalm 23. I have not been told why but I will be obedient. It is vitally important to be

obedient when you hear the Holy Spirit speak. Most of the time, it

will be an inner voice which is not against the word of God. God

will not contradict his word. He can speak audibly to you. I heard

his audible voice once. It is an awe-inspiring experience. Once you

hear the audible voice of God, you are forever changed.

> He that dwelleth in the secret place of the Most
> High shall abide under the shadow of the Almighty.
> I will say of the LORD, He is my refuge and my
> fortress: my God; in Him will I trust. Surely, He
> shall deliver thee from the snare of the fowler, and
> from the noisome pestilence. He shall cover thee
> with his feathers, and under his wings shalt thou
> trust: His truth shall be thy shield and buckler. Thou
> shalt not be afraid for the terror by night; nor for
> the arrow that flieth by day; Nor for the pestilence
> that walketh in darkness; nor for the destruction
> that wasteth at noonday. A thousand shall fall at thy
> side, and ten thousand at thy right hand; but it shall
> not come nigh thee. Only with thine eyes shalt thou
> behold and see the reward of the wicked. Because
> thou hast made the LORD, which is my refuge, even
> the Most High, thy habitation; There shall no evil
> befall thee, neither shall any plague come nigh
> thy dwelling. For He shall give His angels charge
> over thee, to keep thee in all thy ways. They shall
> bear thee up in their hands, lest thou dash thy foot
> against a stone. Thou shalt tread upon the lion and
> adder: the young lion and the dragon shalt thou
> trample under feet. Because He hath set His love
> upon me, therefore will I deliver Him: I will set
> Him on high, because He hath known my name. He
> shall call upon me, and I will answer Him: I will be

with Him in trouble; I will deliver Him, and honour Him. With long life will I satisfy Him and shew Him my salvation.

Psalm 91 (KJV)

The LORD is my shepherd; I shall not want. He maketh me to lie down in green pastures: He leadeth me beside the still waters. He restoreth my soul: He leadeth me in the paths of righteousness for His name's sake. Yea, though I walk through the valley of the shadow of death, I will fear no evil: for thou art with me; thy rod and thy staff they comfort me. Thou preparest a table before me in the presence of mine enemies: thou anointest my head with oil; my cup runneth over. Surely goodness and mercy shall follow me all the days of my life: and I will dwell in the house of the LORD FOREVER.

Psalm 23 (KJV)

Important ideas, Notes, and Words to clarify:

_____

_____

_____

_____

_____

_____

_____

_____

_____

Sherry Grandfield

Step 7: Read the Bible and Reread

This is where the power lies. True power is in the word of God. This is the only book with documented studies showing that reading it will change your very DNA. Perhaps other people realize that, and that is the underlying reason there are attempts to keep people from reading it around the world, even with threats of death. Ask yourself: if this was just an ordinary book why would that be necessary?

The more you read this book, The Bible, the healthier you will become. Pay attention here, I did not say the more time you spend in church and doing church activities the healthier you will become. The Word, and reading it and saying it, is what heals and strengthens your body. The more you read it, the more you will walk in the supernatural. The more you read it, the clearer you will hear the voice of the Holy Spirit telling you which way to go, what decision to make, where to go and where to stay away from, who

to talk to and who to avoid. It is amazing!

> My son, pay attention to my words *and* be willing
> to learn; Open your ears to my sayings. Do not
> let them escape from your sight; Keep them in
> the center of your heart. For they are life to those
> who find them, And healing *and* health to all their
> flesh. Watch over your heart with all diligence,
> For from it *flow* the springs of life. Put away from
> you a deceitful (lying, misleading) mouth, And
> put devious lips far from you. Let your eyes look
> directly ahead [toward the path of moral courage]
> And let your gaze be fixed straight in front of you
> [toward the path of integrity].
> Consider well *and* watch carefully the path of your
> feet, And all your ways will be steadfast *and* sure.
> Do not turn away to the right nor to the left [where
> evil may lurk]; Turn your foot from [the path of]
> evil.
>
> Proverbs 4:20-27 (AMP)

Your ears will hear a word behind you, "This is the

way, walk in it," whenever you turn to the right or

to the left. And you will defile your carved images

overlaid with silver, and your cast images plated with

gold. You will scatter them like a bloodstained *cloth*,

and will say to them, "Begone!" Then He will give

you rain for the seed with which you sow the ground,

and bread [grain] from the produce of the ground, and

it will be rich and plentiful. In that day your livestock
will graze in large *and* roomy pastures (Isaiah 30:21-
23, AMP).

The Bible has been under attack from the beginning. The
kingdom suffereth violence but the violent take it by force. While
typing this, my computer just spoke to me out loud (never did that
before in the three years I've owned it) and said "Always scan
this section" so it must be important---weird occurrences of the
supernatural.

Important ideas, Notes, and Words to clarify:

_____

_____

_____

_____

_____

_____

_____

_____

_____

_____

_____

_____

Step Eight: Take Communion Daily

This chapter was not in my original outline. However, I know when I hear God's voice. He wants you to understand the importance of Communion and why we should honor him in this way on a daily basis. Some of you may have heard of Communion, some of you may have taken Communion at your church, and some of you are thinking "What is this lady talking about?" Hahaha…that's okay. I am going to spell it out for you – or rather spill it out – on these pages for easy understanding.

During what is called "The Last Supper," right before Jesus was crucified, this is what happened and what Jesus said to his disciples:

> Now as they were eating Jesus took bread, and after blessing it, He broke it and gave it to the disciples, and said, "Take, eat; this is My body." And when He had taken a cup and given thanks, He gave

it to them, saying, "Drink from it, all of you; for this is My blood of the [new and better] covenant, which [ratifies the agreement and] is being poured out for many [as a substitutionary atonement] for the forgiveness of sins. But I say to you, I will not drink of this fruit of the vine from now on until that day when I drink it new with you in My Father's Kingdom."

Matthew 26:26-29 (AMP)

This is incredible to me! Jesus told his disciples he would wait until they all arrived in the Kingdom of God before he would have another glass of wine. Imagine giving up a favorite drink or food for a long while – many, many years. Okay, now back to what is Communion.

Communion is defined at MerriamWebster.com as the act or instance of sharing. So, what exactly are we sharing? We are sharing a spiritual interchange of total healing, physically and spiritually in our mortal bodies. This is because of what took place when Jesus died on the cross. This is confirmed in scripture as: "… so that He fulfilled what was spoken by the prophet Isaiah: 'HE HIMSELF TOOK OUR INFIRMITIES [upon Himself] AND CARRIED AWAY OUR DISEASES'" (Matthew 8:17, AMP).

But [in fact] He has borne our griefs, And He has carried our sorrows *and* pains; Yet we [ignorantly] assumed that He was stricken, Struck down by God and degraded *and* humiliated [by Him]. But He was

wounded for our transgressions,
He was crushed for our wickedness [our sin,
our injustice, our wrongdoing]; The punishment
[required] for our well-being *fell* on Him, And
by His stripes (wounds) we are healed. All of us
like sheep have gone astray, We have turned, each
one, to his own way; But the LORD has caused the
wickedness of us all [our sin, our injustice, our
wrongdoing] To fall on Him [instead of us].

Isaiah 6:4-6 (AMP)

Communion = Fellowship = Solidifying your relationship with

Jesus

Essentially, Communion is the glue that makes what He did on

the cross fully accessible. His incorruptible body heals our flesh

through this interchange. His blood heals our soul and spirit and,

in the process, changes our very DNA. The words in Psalm 99

describe how we should consider when we take Communion.

The LORD reigns, let the peoples tremble [with
submissive wonder]! He sits enthroned above the
cherubim, let the earth shake! The LORD is great
in Zion, And He is exalted *and* magnified above
all the peoples. Let them [reverently] praise Your
great and awesome name; Holy is He. The strength
of the King loves justice *and* righteous judgment;
You have established fairness; You have executed
justice and righteousness in Jacob (Israel). Exalt
the LORD our God And worship at His footstool;
Holy is He. Moses and Aaron were among His
priests, And Samuel was among those who called
on His name; They called upon the LORD and He

answered them. He spoke to them in the pillar of cloud; They kept His testimonies And the statutes that He gave them. You answered them, O LORD our God; You were a forgiving God to them, And yet an avenger of their *evil* practices. Exalt the LORD our God And worship at His holy hill [Zion, the temple mount], For the LORD our God is holy.

Psalm 99 (AMP)

Communion, when discerned properly, is the highest form of worship we can offer. Jesus wants us to understand and acknowledge what He went through for us and our redemption. We must no longer do this as a ritual without thinking or without a true understanding. When even one of us takes Communion properly, this makes Jesus smile. Let's do this thing right for Jesus, our Father, and the Holy Spirit.

"Christ purchased our freedom *and* redeemed us from the curse of the Law *and* its condemnation by becoming a curse for us— for it is written, 'CURSED IS EVERYONE WHO HANGS [crucified] ON A TREE (cross)'" (Galatians 3:13, AMP).

Your questions now might be "How do we *actually* take Communion? What does this *look* like?" Well, let's talk about Apostle Paul and his instruction on Communion.

For anyone who eats and drinks [without solemn reverence and heartfelt gratitude for the sacrifice of

Christ], eats and drinks a judgment on himself if he does not recognize the body [of Christ]. That [careless and unworthy participation] is the reason why many among you are weak and sick, and a number sleep [in death].

I Corinthians 11:29-30 (AMP)

Apostle Paul spoke about being careful to not eat the bread and drink the cup unworthily. In the church, you may learn to ask for forgiveness of all sin that you may have committed since the last Communion or in general. Asking for forgiveness is always a good practice and necessary but, Apostle Paul ventured a bit deeper. God wants us to be healthy, healed and whole, not sickly, as mentioned by Apostle Paul.

In summary, when taking Communion, recognize our God's holiness, be grateful beyond words and accept the exchange of His perfect sacrifice for our redemption into your mortal body. Read and reread Psalm 99 to receive a better understanding of our posture with God. He is King of kings and Lord of lords. He loves us, He is Holy, He is our Creator.

There are three necessary elements for Communion: The Bread, The Wine and the cup of some sort. The bread can be a piece of crust, a large chunk of Italian bread, a cracker, a piece of matzah, an actual Communion wafer, any type of "bread" you have available. The wine can be any drink made with grapes (if none is available, then just use water or however the Lord leads you). The cup can be a beautiful jewel ordained goblet, a beautiful glass, or if all you have is a paper cup, use what you have. God knows your heart. Most people recite the words of Jesus from Matthew 26: 26-29 as they practice Communion as below:

> Now as they were eating Jesus took bread, and after blessing it, He broke it and gave it to the disciples, and said, "Take, eat; this is My body."

> (Eat the Bread)

> And when He had taken a cup and given thanks, He gave it to them, saying, "Drink from it, all of you; for this is My blood of the [new and better] covenant, which [ratifies the agreement and] is being poured out for many [as a substitutionary atonement] for the forgiveness of sins.

> (Drink the wine)

> But I say to you, I will not drink of this fruit of the vine from now on until that day when I drink it new with you in My Father's kingdom."

> Matthew 26:26-29 (AMP)

Be blessed and be healthy. Take Communion daily; even more than once a day would be awesome! Hallelujah Jesus, we do not have to be in a church service to take Communion.

Spiritual Warfare for Kingdom Kids

Important ideas, Notes, and Words to clarify:

_____

_____

_____

_____

_____

_____

_____

_____

_____

_____

_____

_____

_____

_____

_____

_____

_____

_____

_____

_____

_____

Step 9: Learn to Walk in Obedience

How well do you follow directions? How much do you hesitate, before you follow through and do as you are directed? Are you a procrastinator?

> Has the LORD as great a delight in burnt offerings and sacrifices
> As in obedience to the voice of the LORD?
> Behold, to obey is better than sacrifice,
> And to heed [is better] than the fat of rams.
>
> 1 Samuel 15:22 (AMP)

According to Merriam-webster.com the word "heed" means to pay attention or notice. In essence, God would much rather that we obey his word and his voice, than to have an offering of money, time, or service that he didn't tell us to do. The voice of the Lord must be heard clearly and followed without hesitation. This is so very important! In some situations, not following God's voice could cost you your very life.

> Do everything without murmuring or questioning [the providence of God], so that you may prove yourselves to be blameless *and* guileless, innocent *and* uncontaminated, children of God without blemish in the midst of a [morally] crooked and [spiritually] perverted generation, among whom you are seen as bright lights [beacons shining out clearly] in the world [of darkness], holding out *and* offering to everyone the word of life, so that in the day of Christ I will have reason to rejoice greatly because I did not run [my race] in vain nor labor without result.
>
> Philippians 2:14-16 (AMP)

Often you will not even be allowed to communicate what the Lord has shown you to others. You may not be able to tell anyone what you're doing or why you are doing it. God may tell you to stay quiet and keep things to yourself. People may be angry with you or call you more than extra, over the top, and say you are exaggerating. We must not be concerned about the comments of family, friends, or associates. We must not be concerned if they like us or not. Our only goal must be to hear "Well done my good and faithful servant" when we stand before God and enter into eternity.

Currently, I am working in the customer service industry. I

like my job well enough, but recently there have been quite a few changes. Many people have left to work elsewhere. I have been looking at other options as well, but I sharply hear the voice of the Lord, "Sit tight," so I will not move until God shows me or tells me what step to take next.

You are asking "How do I know it's God speaking to me?" I will say practice makes perfect, as the enemy tries to speak to us too. Our creator loves us and wants to communicate with us so very much. Just ask God a question, and then ask him to show you the answer in his word, in a vision or a dream. Then wait.

Sometimes he will give you a scripture to read. You will just have an inner inkling to go read scripture similar to Romans 8:3 and when you read it, there will be your answer. Sometimes it will be a picture in your mind or a dream that will contain just the right answer. The process could take a few minutes, hours, or even weeks, but rest assured, God will answer.

As you practice this way of learning to hear God, his voice will become clearer and more recognizable to you. God will not contradict or go against what is written in the Bible. His word is your litmus test for what you believe you are hearing. God will even speak to you about simple things.

Often, I am directed on which route to take to go to work or an appointment. The way I am advised to go may, in fact, be longer than usual. I heed the voice of the Lord; I listen and obey. One day I was told to stay home from work. That day there was a shooting outside my school and a bullet actually hit my classroom window, although it did not break the tempered glass. However, all the teachers and students were stuck there and on lockdown until 10 p. m.

My daughter was in middle school at the time, and I the only parent. God ensured that I was safe and home with my child. Thank you, Jesus, that you watch over us! Hallelujah to the lamb that was slain for us! So yes, God is concerned for our safety and even the smallest details of our lives. Many people have spoken of how they survived 9/11 in this manner. Yes, God can advise us to stay home from work, school or any activity to avoid tragedy.

He is a good Father. The more we let him in, the more he will show us great and wonderful things. He so wants a real relationship with each one of us. Each one of us has a book written about us in Heaven with all we are meant to accomplish during our time here on earth.

"Your eyes have seen my unformed substance; and in Your book were all written the days that were appointed me, when as yet there was not one of them [even taking shape]" (Psalm 139:16, AMP).

I want to complete everything in my book; I don't want to miss any detail. I am sure you are excited to do everything in your book. Remember, God is in charge of time, so if you feel you are a little behind in getting started, it is okay. God can accelerate you.

Be obedient. Be obedient. Be obedient. Be blessed. Be blessed. Be blessed. The blessings of God result from our obedience to him. There will be tests, trials, and tribulations. We must regard ourselves as soldiers and continue to advance forward for the will of God. We must keep our eyes on Jesus, and not on our circumstances.

> Praise the LORD! (Hallelujah!) Blessed [fortunate, prosperous, and favored by God] is the man who fears the LORD [with awe-inspired reverence and worships Him with obedience], Who delights greatly in His commandments. His descendants will be mighty on earth; The generation of the upright will be blessed. Wealth and riches are in his house, And his righteousness endures forever.
>
> Psalm 112:1-3 (AMP)

This Psalm makes it clear that the blessing of God includes

wealth. You will hear people say that Christians should not have wealth; that is a lie from the pit of hell. Of course, we should have money, so we are free to do the work of God without struggle. Jesus came so we could have life and have it more abundantly.

"The thief comes only in order to steal, and kill, and destroy. I came that they may have and enjoy life, and have it in abundance [to the full, till it overflows]" (John 10:10, AMP).

Jesus did not come and go through dying on the cross for his children to live a life of poverty and mediocrity. Be obedient and be blessed.

Jesus said, "If you [really] love Me, you will keep and obey My Commandments" (John 14:15, AMP).

Jesus said:

> Do not think that I came to do away with or undo the Law [of Moses} or the [writing of the] Prophets; I did not come to destroy but to fulfill. For I assure you and most solemnly say to you, until Heaven and earth pass away, not the smallest letter or stroke [of the pen] will pass from the Law until all the things [which it foreshows] are accomplished. So, whoever breaks one of the least [important] of these commandments, and teaches others to do the same, will be called least [important] in the Kingdom of Heaven; but whoever practices and teaches them, he will be called great in the Kingdom of Heaven. For I say to you that unless

your righteousness (uprightness, moral essence is more than that of the Scribes and Pharisees, you will never enter the Kingdom of Heaven.

Matthew 5:17-20 (AMP)

The easiest place to start is to read the Ten Commandments, and there is your basis for obedience. The Ten Commandments are found in the Book of Exodus Chapter 20:

1. You shall have no other gods before me.
2. You shall make no idols.
3. You shall not take the name of the Lord your God in vain.
4. Keep the Sabbath day holy.
5. Honor your father and your mother.
6. You shall not murder.
7. You shall not commit adultery.
8. You shall not steal.
9. You shall not bear false witness against your neighbor.
10. You shall not covet.

Jesus also said, "This is My commandment, that you love and unselfishly seek the best for one another, just as I have loved you" (John 15:12, AMP).

In order to understand the love of Jesus, we must move on to reading about Jesus in the New Testament. We must read Matthew, Mark, Luke, and John over and over until the words of Jesus permeate in our spirits and begin coming out of our mouths. Immerse yourself in the words of Jesus, The Anointed One, and you will become an obedient, trustworthy, and very blessed child of God.

Sherry Grandfield

Important ideas, Notes, and Words to clarify:

Step 10: Encourage Yourself

There will be times throughout your life when you may feel alone, that you are misunderstood or maybe you missed it and are off your correct path to destiny. It is in these times that we must especially pay attention and encourage ourselves to move forward. One of the best ways to do this is to meditate on the word of God. There are thousands of uplifting words from our Beloved Creator in the Bible.

One of my favorites is Isaiah Chapter 60 from start to finish. I love this Chapter and I hope you will too.

> Arise [from spiritual depression to a new life],
> shine [be radiant with the glory *and* brilliance
> of the LORD]; for your light has come, And the
> glory *and* brilliance of the LORD has risen upon
> you. For in fact, darkness will cover the earth
> And deep darkness *will cover* the peoples; But
> the LORD will rise upon you [Jerusalem] And His
> glory *and* brilliance will be seen on you. Nations

will come to your light, And kings to the brightness of your rising. Lift up your eyes around you and see; They all gather together, they come to you. Your sons will come from far away, And your daughters will be looked after at *their* side. Then you will see and be radiant, And your heart will tremble [with joy] and rejoice Because the abundant wealth of the seas will [a]be brought to you, The wealth of the nations will come to you. A multitude of camels [from the eastern trading tribes] will cover you [Jerusalem], The young camels of Midian and Ephah; All those from Sheba [who once came to trade] will come Bringing gold and frankincense And proclaiming the praises of the Lord. All the flocks of Kedar will be gathered to you [as the eastern pastoral tribes join the trading tribes], The rams of Nebaioth will serve you; They will go up with acceptance [as sacrifices] on My altar, And I will glorify the house of My honor *and* splendor. Who are these who fly like a cloud And like doves to their windows? The islands *and* coastlands will confidently wait for Me; And the ships of Tarshish *will come* first, To bring your sons from far away, Their silver and gold with them, For the name of the Lord your God, For the Holy One of Israel because He has glorified you. Foreigners will build up your walls, And their kings will serve you; For in My [righteous] wrath I struck you, But in My favor *and* grace, I have had compassion on you. Your gates will be open continually; They shall not be shut day or night, So that people may bring to you the wealth of the nations—With their kings led in procession. For the nation or the kingdom which will not serve you [Jerusalem] shall perish, And the nations [that refuse to serve] shall be utterly ruined. The glory of Lebanon will come to you, The cypress, the juniper, and the cedar together,

To beautify the place of My sanctuary; And I will honor *and* make the place of My feet glorious. The sons of those who oppressed you will come bowing down to you [in submission], And all those who despised you *and* treated you disrespectfully will bow down at the soles of your feet, And they will call you the City of the LORD, The Zion of the Holy One of Israel. Whereas you [Jerusalem] have been abandoned and hated With no one passing through, I will make you an object of pride forever, A joy from generation to generation. You will suck the milk of the [Gentile] nations
And suck the breast (abundance) of kings; Then you will recognize *and* know that I, the LORD, am your Savior And your Redeemer, the Mighty One of Jacob. Instead of bronze, I will bring gold, And instead of iron, I will bring silver, And instead of wood, bronze, And instead of stones, iron. And [instead of the tyranny of the present] I will appoint peace as your officers, And righteousness your rulers. Violence will not be heard again in your land, Nor devastation or destruction within your borders; But you will call your walls Salvation, and your gates Praise [to God]. The sun will no longer be your light by day, Nor shall the bright glow of the moon give light to you, But the LORD will be an everlasting light for you; And your God will be your glory *and* splendor. Your sun will no longer set, Nor will your moon wane; For the LORD will be your everlasting light,
And the days of your mourning will be over. Then all your people will be [uncompromisingly and consistently] righteous; They will possess the land forever, The branch of My planting, The work of My hands, That I may be glorified. The smallest one will become a thousand (a clan), And the least one a mighty nation. I, the LORD, will quicken it in its

[appointed] time.

Isaiah 60 (AMP)

There will also be times in your life when God is transitioning you to something new. The "something new" can come in many forms: a new school, a move to another place to live, a new career… Sometimes the change does not appear to be what we would want or desire. It is at that moment when we think "Oh, I don't think I would want that." We need to latch on to the knowledge that our God is a good Father and He loves us.

"And we know [with great confidence] that God [who is deeply concerned about us] causes all things to work together [as a plan] for good for those who love God, to those who are called according to His plan *and* purpose" (Romans 8:28, AMP).

We must be like Apostle Paul when he stated:

"I press on toward the goal to win the [heavenly] prize of the upward call of God in Christ Jesus" (Philippians 3:14, AMP).

So, greet each day with the mindset of the focusing on the fruits of the spirit.

But the fruit of the Spirit [the result of His presence

within us] is love [unselfish concern for others], joy, [inner] peace, patience [not the ability to wait, but how we act while waiting], kindness, goodness, faithfulness, gentleness, self-control. Against such things, there is no law.

Galatians 5:22-23 (AMP)

Below you will find some short prayers to edify your spirit and keep you encouraged. These prayers were given to me by some very dear friends who are strong Word people. They are delighted that I am sharing them with you. It is recommended that you focus on one a week and when you are through, begin again. I have found this to be quite helpful. Also, you can pray this for others too, just substitute their name instead of my in each line. God bless you always.

Weekly Fruit of the Spirit Prayers

Week 1: In the Name of Jesus, the Anointed One and His Anointing, I speak the fruit of love into my spirit, soul, and body.

Week 2: In the Name of Jesus, the Anointed One and His Anointing, I speak the fruit of joy into my spirit, soul, and body.

Week 3: In the Name of Jesus, the Anointed One and His Anointing, I speak the fruit of peace into my spirit, soul, and body.

Week 4: In the Name of Jesus, the Anointed One and His

Anointing, I speak the fruit of patience into my spirit, soul, and body.

Week 5: In the Name of Jesus, the Anointed One and His Anointing, I speak the fruit of kindness into my spirit, soul, and body.

Week 6: In the Name of Jesus, the Anointed One and His Anointing, I speak the fruit of goodness into my spirit, soul, and body.

Week 7: In the Name of Jesus, the Anointed One and His Anointing, I speak the fruit of faithfulness into my spirit, soul, and body.

Week 8: In the Name of Jesus, the Anointed One and His Anointing, I speak the fruit of gentleness into my spirit, soul, and body.

Week 9: In the Name of Jesus, the Anointed One and His Anointing, I speak the fruit of self-control into my spirit, soul, and body.

Be Blessed. Be encouraged. Onward and Upward!

Blessed [gratefully praised and adored] be the God and Father of our Lord Jesus Christ, the

Father of mercies and the God of all comfort, who comforts *and* encourages us in every trouble so that we will be able to comfort *and* encourage those who are in any kind of trouble, with the comfort with which we ourselves are comforted by God.

2 Corinthians 1:3-4 (AMP)

Important ideas, Notes, and Words to clarify:

_____

_____

_____

_____

_____

_____

_____

_____

_____

_____

_____

_____

_____

_____

_____

_____

Sherry Grandfield

62

Step 11: Fulfill the Great Commission

This is where the rubber meets the road. This is the tipping point. Here is where many do not embark or choose to participate, but this is part of being a true follower and disciple of Christ. Let's read the scripture below from the Book of Mark for a little background.

> Later, Jesus appeared to the eleven [disciples] themselves as they were reclining *at the table*; and He called them to account for their unbelief and hardness of heart because they had not believed those who had seen Him after He had risen [from death]. And He said to them, "Go into all the world and preach the gospel to all creation. He who has believed [in Me] and has been baptized will be saved [from the penalty of God's wrath and judgment]; but he who has not believed will be condemned. These signs will accompany those who have believed: in My name, they will cast out demons, they will speak in new tongues; they will pick up serpents, and if they drink anything deadly, it will not hurt them; they will lay

hands on the sick, and they will get well.

Mark 16:14-18 (AMP)

So, you see at the end, the scripture talks about casting out demons? I have heard so, many people who go to church, even Pastors, who have told me that casting out demons is not their call. Jesus never split the Great Commission in parts. In fact, Jesus actually did say:

"I assure you *and* most solemnly say to you, anyone who believes in Me [as Savior] will also do the things that I do; and he will do even greater things than these [in extent and outreach], because I am going to the Father" (John 14:12, AMP).

After Jesus resurrected from the dead and appeared to his disciples this is what he said:

> Now the eleven disciples went to Galilee, to the mountain which Jesus had designated. And when they saw Him, they worshiped *Him*; but some doubted [that it was really He]. Jesus came up and said to them, "All authority (all power of absolute rule) in Heaven and on earth has been given to Me. Go therefore and make disciples of all the nations [help the people to learn of Me, believe in Me, and obey My words], baptizing them in the name of the Father and of the Son and of the Holy Spirit, teaching them to observe everything that I have commanded you; and lo, I am with you always [remaining with you perpetually—regardless of circumstance, and on

every occasion], even to the end of the age.

Matthew 28:16-20 (AMP)

Jesus did not mince words or speak lightly about what his instructions were and still remain today. I believe that we must be able to do what Jesus did to be able to do the greater works. Doesn't that make sense to you?

"Jesus summoned His twelve disciples and gave them authority *and* power over unclean spirits, to cast them out, and to heal every kind of disease and every kind of sickness" (Matthew 10:1, AMP).

Healing the sick, opening the eyes of the blind, seeing the lame walk, all of this is possible for those who believe. So, if we have completed steps 1-11, then please consider the resources in the Appendix. Read Matthew, Mark, Luke, and John repeatedly. Choose a resource and watch some videos on a topic of interest to you, read material from the websites, listen to audio recordings.

There are no limitations as to how far you can go with God. Take a step towards God and he will not only meet you, but he will lift you up higher than you ever imagined. May God bless and protect you and all your concerns. May you rest in God and have peace going forth as a mighty warrior for the Kingdom of God in

Sherry Grandfield

power, strength, and divine health in Jesus' Name, Amen.

Important ideas, Notes, and Words to clarify:

_____

_____

_____

_____

_____

_____

_____

_____

_____

_____

_____

_____

_____

_____

_____

_____

_____

After you read Assessment

I always like to figure out what I know about something new before I read about it. After I read about what used to be new, I then like to see what I learned. This is called an ABC list and it's an easy way to see your growth at the end of the reading. List all the letters of the alphabet down the side of a paper or in two columns. Think about the title of this book: Spiritual Warfare for Kingdom Kids. Write one word that starts with each letter of the alphabet that you think relates to the title. If you can't think of one, leave it blank. This should only take about 15 minutes or less. When you have completed this list compare it to the answers to the one before you read the book. I am sure you have learned a lot. Congratulations!

A_____

B_____

C_____

D_____

E_____

F_____

G_____

H_____

I _____

J _____

K_____

L_____

M_____

N_____

O_____

P _____

Q_____

R_____

S _____

T_____

U_____

V_____

W_____

X_____

Y_____

Z _____

Sherry Grandfield

APPENDIX

Websites

1. Annwindsor.com (Ann Windsor)
2. awni.net (Andrew Wommack)
3. billyburke.org (Billy Burke)
4. beinhealth.com (Henry Wright)
5. charlescarrin.com (Charles Carrin)
6. cappsministries.com (Charles Capps)
7. thegloryzone.org (David and Stephanie Herzog)
8. dondickerman.com (Don Dickerman)
9. frankmarzullo.com (Frank Marzullo)
10. familyfoundations.com (Craig Hill)
11. healingrooms.com (International Association of Healing Rooms)
12. harbourchurch.org (Harbour Church)
13. hbcdelivers.org (Hegewisch Baptist Church)
14. jdm.org (Jesse Duplantis)
15. johnramirez.org (John Ramirez)
16. kcm.org (Kenneth and Gloria Copeland)
17. kevinzadai.com (Kevin Zadai)
18. kingjesusmiami.org (King Jesus Ministries)
19. drlestersumrall.com (Lester Sumrall)
20. newwinemin.com (New Wine Ministries)
21. healingroomsministries.com (Rich and Dottie Kane)
22. repentancerevival.com (Robert Clancy)
23. omegamanradio.com (Shannon Davis)
24. sidroth.org (Sid Roth)
25. smithwigglesworth.com (Smith Wigglesworth)
26. taklife.org (Temple Aaron Hakodesh)
27. tbn.org (Trinity Broadcasting Network)
28. wordsoflife.com (Words of Life Church)

Sherry Grandfield

Music and Media

1. Al Hobbs
2. Andrew and Mary Kat Ehrenzeller
3. Bethel Music
4. Cece Winans
5. David and Nicole Binion
6. Eddie James
7. Fred Hammond
8. God's Property
9. Hezekiah Walker
10. Hillsong
11. Justin Jarvis
12. Kevin Zadai
13. Kirk Franklin
14. Marvin Sapp
15. Micah Stampley
16. New Life Community Church
17. Naida Lynn Alcime
18. Paul Wilbur
19. Rick Pino
20. Tilda Paris
21. Vertical Worship
22. Vicki Yohe
23. wpfilm.com (director/producer Darren Wilson)
24. worshipmob.com (director/producer Sean Mulholland)
25. www.publications.com

Sherry Grandfield

CPSIA information can be obtained
at www.ICGtesting.com
Printed in the USA
BVHW090719130422
634146BV00010B/197